Set design by Douglas Stein. Photo by Joan Marcus

A scene from the Playwrights Horizons production of *Boys and Girls*.

BOYS AND GIRLS
BY TOM DONAGHY

DRAMATISTS
PLAY SERVICE
INC.

BOYS AND GIRLS
Copyright © 2003, Tom Donaghy

All Rights Reserved

CAUTION: Professionals and amateurs are hereby warned that performance of BOYS AND GIRLS is subject to payment of a royalty. It is fully protected under the copyright laws of the United States of America, and of all countries covered by the International Copyright Union (including the Dominion of Canada and the rest of the British Commonwealth), and of all countries covered by the Pan-American Copyright Convention, the Universal Copyright Convention, the Berne Convention, and of all countries with which the United States has reciprocal copyright relations. All rights, including professional/amateur stage rights, motion picture, recitation, lecturing, public reading, radio broadcasting, television, video or sound recording, all other forms of mechanical or electronic reproduction, such as CD-ROM, CD-I, DVD, information storage and retrieval systems and photocopying, and the rights of translation into foreign languages, are strictly reserved. Particular emphasis is placed upon the matter of readings, permission for which must be secured from the Author's agent in writing.

The English language stock and amateur stage performance rights in the United States, its territories, possessions and Canada for BOYS AND GIRLS are controlled exclusively by DRAMATISTS PLAY SERVICE, INC., 440 Park Avenue South, New York, NY 10016. No professional or nonprofessional performance of the Play may be given without obtaining in advance the written permission of DRAMATISTS PLAY SERVICE, INC., and paying the requisite fee.

Inquiries concerning all other rights should be addressed to International Creative Management, Inc., 40 West 57th Street, New York, NY 10019. Attn: Sarah Jane Leigh.

SPECIAL NOTE
Anyone receiving permission to produce BOYS AND GIRLS is required to give credit to the Author as sole and exclusive Author of the Play on the title page of all programs distributed in connection with performances of the Play and in all instances in which the title of the Play appears for purposes of advertising, publicizing or otherwise exploiting the Play and/or a production thereof. The name of the Author must appear on a separate line, in which no other name appears, immediately beneath the title and in size of type equal to 50% of the size of the largest, most prominent letter used for the title of the Play. No person, firm or entity may receive credit larger or more prominent than that accorded the Author. The following acknowledgments must appear on the title page in all programs distributed in connection with performances of the Play:

Playwrights Horizons, Inc., New York City, produced the World Premiere of *Boys and Girls* Off-Broadway in 2002.

Boys and Girls was originally presented as a workshop by New York Stage and Film Company and The Powerhouse Theater at Vassar in June 2001.

Originally commissioned by South Coast Repertory.

for Kate

AUTHOR'S NOTE

To the directors and actors who might tackle this play:

Make sure these people are played with generosity. They aren't arguing with each other or battling it out. They are trying their best to fix and complete their lives. They are aware of their foibles and know they can behave ridiculously. This makes them smile at themselves and each other more often than the script suggests.

Thanks,
Tom Donaghy

BOYS AND GIRLS was originally presented as a workshop by New York Stage and Film Company (Mark Linn-Baker, Max Mayer, Johanna Pfaelzer and Leslie Urdang, Producing Directors) and The Powerhouse Theater at Vassar (Beth Fargis-Lancaster, Executive Producer) in June 2001. The production stage manager was Jennifer Grutza. The cast was as follows:

REED .... Mike Doyle
JASON .... Jeff Whitty
BEV .... Nadia Dajani
SHELLY .... Elizabeth Hanly Rice

BOYS AND GIRLS was originally produced by Playwrights Horizons (Tim Sanford, Artistic Director; Leslie Marcus, Managing Director; William Russo, General Manager) at The Duke Theater in New York City on May 28, 2002. It was directed by Gerald Gutierrez; the set design was by Douglas Stein; the lighting design was by David Weiner; the sound design was by Aural Fixation; the costume design was by Catherine Zuber; and the production stage manager was Marjorie Horne. The cast was as follows:

REED .... Robert Sella
JASON .... Malcolm Gets
BEV .... Nadia Dajani
SHELLY .... Carrie Preston

CHARACTERS

REED
JASON
BEV
SHELLY

SETTING

ACT ONE
A bar.
A duplex apartment.
A studio apartment.

ACT TWO
A beach.
A motel.
An office.
The duplex apartment.
A suite of rented rooms.

BOYS AND GIRLS

ACT ONE

Late August. A bar. A martini shaker and two martini glasses sit on a cafe table flanked by two bar stools. As the lights come up, Jason arrives and greets Reed, who has been waiting for him.

REED. Hi.
JASON. Hi. *(They take each other in.)*
REED. I've lost a little.
JASON. It looks good.
REED. No.
JASON. It's not too much.
REED. People say, "You look so skinny."
JASON. It's not.
REED. You don't want people to think there's something wrong! Which there isn't. *(They smile at each other. Jason looks around.)*
JASON. This is nice.
REED. I found it.
JASON. This neighborhood is someplace I don't get.
REED. I was walking around one day. They have those Cuban drinks. And they have hummus on the tables. Which is gratis. It looks like.
JASON. Did you want to get dinner?
REED. I ate. Or I would.
JASON. I didn't, but I'm not hungry. Probably later. It's only — *(He looks at his watch.)* It's early. *(They sit.)*
REED. Well.

JASON. I know.
REED. I'm glad we can do this!
JASON. Sure.
REED. I am.
JASON. I don't mean "sure" like "sure, whatever." 'Cause I'm glad.
REED. Good. *(They are silent a moment.)*
JASON. What if we had dinner later?
REED. I don't —
JASON. Yeah.
REED. Yeah, I don't know. I've got to be cracking early tomorrow, get going.
JASON. You're right.
REED. Maybe if we weren't —
JASON. Right.
REED. — hadn't planned this —
JASON. Dinner is so huge!
REED. It is! *(They laugh.)* It's a real — you can't get out of dinner once it's in motion! *(They laugh.)* You know, in spite of all our, mm, trouble —
JASON. Trouble?
REED. — the troubles, what we are — this — is very rare. This.
JASON. Me too.
REED. And it kills me. It kills me. It always —
JASON. Let's not —
REED. Right.
JASON. We don't have to get into all that —
REED. I don't want to either. *(They smile. Reed pours their drinks.)* It's my birthday.
JASON. Oh, God, I'm so bad.
REED. That's all right.
JASON. I'm so bad.
REED. What're you supposed to — ?
JASON. I am the worst!
REED. — remember since — please!
JASON. No. Happy birthday.
REED. I'm very old.
JASON. Well.
REED. I got carded last week so I thought "fuck it."

8

JASON. Well, who knows what's old anymore? Plans?
REED. There's a, ah, festival, a music festival up by the house. Ravel. Lots of strings.
JASON. Happy birthday.
REED. Please.
JASON. Hardly old.
REED. It's an outdoor festival. On a, uh, lawn. You bring a picnic dinner, wine. Cheeses.
JASON. It's supposed to be nice this weekend.
REED. It's sunny all weekend, they're saying.
JASON. I saw the news before I came, yeah. *(Beat.)* There's maybe *some* chance of —
REED. — small chance of late afternoon —
JASON. — showers —
REED. — drizzle. *(Beat.)* Only tomorrow, though. So Sunday I'm gonna try and organize everyone up at the house, which will be a challenge because they are constantly stoned. They're growing it in the garden. And it's going in all the food! Everyone's walking around, toppling things. All the crockery's broken. Pieces of everyone's dead grandmother's china. There's all this ice cream, eating it from the box with spoons, too stoned to put it in bowls. There's pot in the salad, everyone's lost their mind. These are Ph.D.'s and they are baked! No one's paid a bill in ages. And I don't understand the books. When we all got the place I was like, "I don't want to be den mother, that's all I ask — I'm through with caretaking!" *(Beat.)* That wasn't directed at you. Or us. None of that was meant to have significance.
JASON. I know.
REED. I'm just —
JASON. I didn't take it that way.
REED. I wanted to see you.
JASON. I just heard it.
REED. That's the thing. Not settle scores.
JASON. I just heard it without subtext.
REED. *(Beat.)* That's forever ago and I don't want to do anything but — for us to be nice —
JASON. Okay.
REED. — and treat each other as well as we always —
JASON. Good.

REED. I feel — I want us to be — nice.
JASON. *(Beat.)* My father finally died.
REED. I know. I heard through people and I —
JASON. It's okay —
REED. — didn't know what to —
JASON. — you know.
REED. Send something — ?
JASON. No, come on. He's been dying forever. And I hated him. *(Beat.)* Come on, please.
REED. No, I —
JASON. I mean — please. I just wanted it noted. *(They sip their martinis.)*
REED. Okay, look, I don't want to be disruptive by calling, but there are so many things that happen, unaccountable, a wrench gets in and all that goes on — and I wonder if — if when we see each other, if we can't feel that together? That thing nothing that's happened to us, our failure, can touch. I'm blathering.
JASON. No.
REED. Do you know?
JASON. It's not like you abandoned me.
REED. Of course.
JASON. No one's abandoned me. I'm not a child.
REED. I didn't. I certainly didn't. It was your choice. You can arrange it any way in your head you want.
JASON. What was?
REED. And I'm sure you have. Self-protectively. But you have had the choice.
JASON. No, it wasn't.
REED. You could've come up to me any moment, at any moment and said, "I've decided to be responsible. I've decided we are grown-ups."
JASON. It was your choice.
REED. "I've decided — " you know, some cliche, "Love saves the day," or some other bumper sticker. Something. You had that choice.
JASON. Fine.
REED. You don't believe it.
JASON. And what would you say?
REED. Well.

JASON. If I did? If I came and said just blah, just all that. You'd say what?
REED. *(Beat.)* I'd say I'd consider it.
JASON. You suck.
REED. No, you do. You really do. *(They laugh at themselves.)*
JASON. I have a present for you. It's just a little —
REED. I thought you forgot — ?
JASON. — I did, but maybe I knew somewhere in the back of my head — *(Jason takes a gift-wrapped book from his bag and puts it on the table.)*
REED. What is it?
JASON. It's a biography.
REED. Can I open it later?
JASON. *(Nods.)* I know you're off biographies, but I think you'll like it. It has perspective.
REED. Someone I admire?
JASON. One of your icons. I know you're off them but this one I thought —
REED. Did you read it first?
JASON. Too many pages. There's no time lately, the hours, I'm stuck dawn to dusk, beyond dusk. A car comes to drive me home, though. And there's always food, ordering in, expense accounts —
REED. Good.
JASON. And I'm being praised for my work. They're being very good to me. And there've been raises. So I can get this.
REED. No.
JASON. I want to.
REED. That's silly.
JASON. No, I'm getting it. It's your birthday, let me pay the bill at least. Please. Come on.
REED. *(Beat.)* I want to talk about something. I don't know how to bring it up gently. Your — sadness, your sadnesses. In the past, your struggles. I'm not with you on a daily basis anymore so —
JASON. You're not.
REED. No, I'm sure —
JASON. *(Over next line.)* If you were you'd know —
REED. — you're fine, you're better, I hope.
JASON. You're not and if you were —

REED. You seem better and I don't know, and I know this is presumptuous, but your last call.
JASON. *(Beat.)* Oh.
REED. You'd been drinking a lot. You said it.
JASON. I know.
REED. You said it and I thought, "I don't want him to."
JASON. I know. And I appreciate it, I do.
REED. That's why I sent that letter.
JASON. I appreciate it, I do. Your concern. I do.
REED. That's why I sent it.
JASON. You're right to — to — to think of me. You are but —
REED. No.
JASON. — but no, you are. As hard as that sounds — to hear. For me. *(Jason sips his drink.)*
REED. I always wanted us to understand each other.
JASON. I do.
REED. And if there's any way, if there's some way you could see there's help. From sadness. There's help.
JASON. It just happens I don't believe in help. Or therapy. Or whatever you're suggesting. And I'm surrounded by people who feel the same way.
REED. And I'm —
JASON. Fine.
REED. — surrounded by —
JASON. I am.
REED. — by people —
JASON. So that's it.
REED. — who feel differently. It's as I said in my letter.
JASON. Fine, fine —
REED. No — !
JASON. — should we get some appetizers?
REED. No. We have hummus.
JASON. *(Beat.)* No, fine, I'm sorry! You got the brunt of it. You got it — go ahead! Those two years, all that, the binges, vent, you're allowed — the lies, that night, I know. I know you have to see those people all the time and how it must be and I'm sorry.
REED. Please understand.
JASON. No, I do, the money —

REED. Please understand.
JASON. I know you think it's impossible, I know you think — because — I know you think —
REED. This has happened to so many other people.
JASON. No, I know you think —
REED. So many others.
JASON. There comes a time when you say "What happened when I was a child no longer matters." I'm not the first or only person to have a wicked father drink himself to death. *(Beat.)* You make a decision. You make a decision. To be done. A few broken bones. To be done. Twenty years ago! I'm sorry. You got the brunt of it. I don't want us to be constantly saying look here, look what you've done and me having to say I'm sorry, I'm sick of it. I don't want to keep setting that up.
REED. I'm not asking for you to keep saying I'm sorry.
JASON. You are.
REED. I'm sick of it too!
JASON. You are, you don't know it.
REED. I'm sick of thinking that's what you'll say! That I'm invested in this dynamic whereby I'm oppressing you and you're poor-little-wronged-little-whoever-you-are whose apologies are never heard. They're heard!
JASON. Fine.
REED. But that's it?
JASON. If they're heard, fine, what else?
REED. Change!
JASON. Change from what?
REED. Some hope —
JASON. Change from what?
REED. Ambivalence, you tell me, conflictedness, I don't know! You tell me you're doing well, you're doing well and so I think — *(Jason stands as if he will leave.)*
JASON. This is so stupid.
REED. I think there might be hope! If you want it. *(Jason starts to go.)*
JASON. This is —
REED. Do you think about us? *(Jason stops.)*
JASON. *(Beat.)* I think, I think there is some, there is something

13

— or — always inside me — or — something you should know, something that inside me will always be maybe something — be maybe be always ambivalent, I think, about being — being — being — loved. *(Beat.)* And I think that's okay. It's okay. *(They are silent a moment.)*
REED. How's the new apartment?
JASON. Fine, good, you know, great. Up six flights, I keep walking and walking. And once you're up, you're up, forget it. Ice cream? Forget it.
REED. I still don't have the number.
JASON. Work's best anyway, the voice mail. That's where I always am anyway. *(Beat.)* I just don't want to be the crazy one. I can't. *(Beat.)* Are you seeing anyone?
REED. No. *(Beat.)* Are you?
JASON. Yeah.
REED. Oh. *(Beat.)* And what's that like?
JASON. Good. It's good. It's very adult.
REED. Good.
JASON. Yeah. *(Beat.)* We're talking about New Year's Eve and there's all this jabber about where to go, different ideas and — what are you doing for New Year's?
REED. Crawling under my bed. You didn't see me at that bar the other night, did you?
JASON. When?
REED. Uh —
JASON. No, when?
REED. Saturday.
JASON. No, where were you?
REED. Sitting by the bar. You came in, the both of you. Your hair was wet. You must've just showered. You kissed each other.
JASON. I'm sorry.
REED. That was him?
JASON. William. *(Beat.)* He's an architect. *(Beat.)* I'm sorry.
REED. You looked so happy.
JASON. I didn't see you.
REED. I ran out.
JASON. I didn't.
REED. I kept saying, "He didn't see me, he's too nearsighted" —

JASON. I'm sorry. I don't —
REED. I was just there.
JASON. — know what I'd do if I saw —
REED. We live in the same city. It's going to happen. And it will keep happening. It will always happen, always, always. *(Beat.)* Would it be impossible for us to not talk? To not talk. Don't you think it's too upsetting sometimes?
JASON. I don't want to not talk.
REED. I don't either. *(Reed looks at his watch as Jason empties the martini shaker into both their glasses.)* I have to meet the girls soon.
JASON. How are they?
REED. Still kickin'.
JASON. Dykes rule. How's Georgie?
REED. This high — *(Indicates Georgie's height.)* They're finishing up their duplex. It has a turret.
JASON. A turret, wow.
REED. I don't envy it anymore, that.
JASON. You don't have to.
REED. What do you mean?
JASON. You have a country place.
REED. I do.
JASON. Things are going well.
REED. They are.
JASON. I think you're tremendous. *(Beat.)* I think you are. *(Beat.)* I should go.
REED. I always want us to have more time, we just get through the anecdotal — *(Jason stands again.)* — and then — are you happy with him? You smiled at him like you were happy.
JASON. I didn't know you were there.
REED. Like you would smile at me.
JASON. It's very adult.
REED. Your hair was wet.
JASON. It was raining.
REED. I think you always thought I was impervious.
JASON. I never thought you —
REED. How could you be ambivalent about me?
JASON. I didn't know this — *(Jason starts off; Reed stands.)*
REED. I was the one supposed to cure you of that. Right? When

you used to pick me up —
JASON. I didn't —
REED. — you lifted me —
JASON. I didn't know any of this.
REED. I'm sorry —
JASON. I have to go.
REED. What we could have again. With some work. Everything! A child? *(Beat.)* What we always talked about? Someone to raise, better than we were. For our, um, extra love. All of it that was left over. That was too much. And I'll work too — I'm not saying you're the only one. I'll work too!
JASON. I — have to go. *(They smile and nod. Jason goes off, and Reed heads for Bev and Shelly's duplex apartment. When he arrives, Shelly shows off the duplex's recent renovation as Bev looks on, sipping a glass of wine.)*
REED. I can't believe what you've done…!
SHELLY. Pretty good.
BEV. It's been hell.
REED. Six months…!
SHELLY. The contractors!
BEV. One tried to commit suicide. Not here. He went home one day after work. And then we got a call from his wife at the hospital saying he couldn't finish the kitchen 'cause he'd OD'd.
SHELLY. Unbelievable.
BEV. Well, we were trying to cut corners.
SHELLY. He came recommended, but you never know.
BEV. You never know.
SHELLY. If there's —
BEV. If there's suicidal depression in those you hire. But he was a few rungs down cost-wise, with the estimate.
REED. I guess you get what you pay for.
SHELLY. That's what we're learning. *(They laugh.)* I have to go over some papers in the other room, then I'll come back to visit. And there's drinks, whatever, in the fridge, help yourself. And there's cheese. And we bought olives — did you get the garlic ones?
BEV. I think —
SHELLY. And there's Stilton.
BEV. Stilton.

SHELLY. And pears.
BEV. Pears.
SHELLY. From the island.
BEV. Incredible.
SHELLY. They're juicy and they're just ripe so they have to go. There's a baguette somewhere too, check the baskets over the cutting board.
REED. I'm fine.
SHELLY. And I think there's a beer in the back of the fridge. *(Shelly exits to a home office.)*
BEV. She's bringing work home. We're set up so she can.
REED. Things are going well.
BEV. Oh — !
REED. It's incredible.
BEV. You wouldn't believe. I mean you wouldn't believe.
REED. This place.
BEV. This place, the dinners.
REED. Six months!
BEV. We're going to Deruta next week. We need a china service.
REED. I never know where you are.
BEV. We're everywhere. I don't know where we are. It's certainly different.
REED. You made it.
BEV. I did.
REED. Your fortitude.
BEV. With help, I did.
REED. Deruta?
BEV. Right? I mean where the fuck is Deruta?
REED. I always knew because of your, whatever, fortitude, or something.
BEV. No.
REED. You always had rich ones.
BEV. But this one I was sure. And we have to keep that in mind. This one I loved. And then the money came. In buckets.
REED. I think Deruta is in Umbria.
BEV. Gobs and gobs. *(Beat.)* You'll make it too. You will. *(Beat.)* I want you to see our new faucets.
REED. I hope so.

BEV. Sure you will. Oh, and there's a sconce I wanted to show you I'm not sure goes. Get your opinion. Before we go out.
REED. We're not here? I brought wine.
BEV. We were gonna be here.
REED. I thought we were here.
SHELLY. *(Off.)* We have reservations at Ferris!
BEV. Big time.
REED. Ferris?! *(Shelly reenters wearing glasses, holding some papers.)*
SHELLY. It's nothing. And you're dressed fine.
BEV. How 'bout it?
REED. I am not dressed fine — !
BEV. You're fine —
REED. I thought you were going to toss some pasta?
BEV. It's your birthday!
SHELLY. A little celebration. And we called Costanza and she's coming over for Georgie —
BEV. We've got things to celebrate — your birthday, all these years. The things we've been through. And look at all of us. Not bad.
SHELLY. I've been —
BEV. No, sir.
SHELLY. I've been jealous of your friendship. I have.
BEV. *(Beat.)* Come on.
SHELLY. But now I'm glad.
BEV. She is.
SHELLY. We're like friends now. That's something to celebrate.
REED. Of course —
SHELLY. We don't know each other as well —
BEV. — not as much history.
SHELLY. But the stories … Sunday nights with the recipes — those summers — stumbling home over each other. Almost dawn. The sun just —
BEV. That big bouncer trailing after us — we'd forgot something. Scarves, my wallet. You left your keys at the piano with that fat chick singing "Memories." The phone numbers we threw away. We could throw off a trail. A pretty good team.
SHELLY. She always said. And I hear them and I wish I'd — known her sooner.
REED. That was forever ago.

BEV. Not so long.
SHELLY. It seems ancient.
BEV. That time with those bar stools and you toppled off and took me with you. They shouldn't put drunks on high bar stools! I hardly drink at all anymore.
SHELLY. 'Cause I'd kill her.
BEV. She would. We grow up.
REED. We do.
SHELLY. We do. I'll kill you though.
REED. *(Beat.)* Where's the little one?
BEV. Down the hall. He's got his own bathroom.
SHELLY. He gets to choose the color.
BEV. He's campaigning for polka dot. I keep telling him it's not a color.
SHELLY. Okay. I just have another to go over, one more thing, and then we're at nine-thirty. Have some food, though — or that beer. I think it's Belgian. And did he see that book? We want to show you this book from Charlotte's imprint. *(Shelly returns to her office.)*
BEV. God, we were children. We were drinking way too much, I put on all that weight.
REED. You look great.
BEV. I'm down twenty.
REED. So am I.
BEV. Lean and mean.
REED. We were kids.
BEV. She's not jealous.
REED. There's something —
BEV. No —
REED. Not on my end. On hers.
BEV. It's history, no —
REED. A feeling.
BEV. It's natural. And it's over. That's when we met and she was wondering — you and I spent all this time together and everyone had to adjust, struggle. There's a little brutality there when love comes into the picture. She's very fond of you, that's the point. Very. She loves who I love. Now she's secure enough to love who I love. There was a little bloodletting there, but that's — of all our

friends — the friends we have everywhere — you stand in a class, a different class. A class apart. We, you know, cherish you. The struggle's over and we're all a little punch drunk, but still standing.
REED. It upsets her that you and I screwed.
BEV. Just twice. Well, what can you do? Do you want to see the sconce now?
REED. I really haven't been drinking that much anymore.
BEV. She knows that.
REED. Those stories get around.
BEV. She knows.
REED. With all the work it's impossible —
BEV. She's just against anything she perceives as a fault. A character fault, a flaw. She's clean and good and she makes me sturdy. I'm not some kid wandering around at dusk with a six-pack anymore. Peeing on sofas. Sleeping with boys. I haven't peed on anyone's sofa in ten years!
REED. Sure I'll see the sconce. *(He moves to go; Bev doesn't follow.)* What?
BEV. We want you to live with us. *(A moment passes in silence.)*
REED. What?
BEV. He needs a father.
REED. Who? *(Another silence.)* Is he asleep?
BEV. He's asleep now, yeah. He usually goes down around nine. We're trying to make it earlier and tonight he fell for it. He's got this little doll, this monkey if you dangle it long enough it has a hypnotic effect. *(Beat.)* He's four — he knows everything. He knows the whole setup, so it's not an illusion, to create one — a father or a male — he's asking about men. What they're like when they're around. Not for sports or jockey things — but how they're different. He's got all these women and he's great and they love him but there's something else. He knows it.
REED. We've been through this way back.
BEV. No, that was different, that was sperm!
REED. Yes, and it's not mine!
BEV. Shell thinks we have to do something. And I'm in agreement. All around. You look in his eyes and you want to answer that. *(Looks into her wine glass.)* I'm having more, how are you?
REED. Fine.

BEV. You don't want that beer?
REED. No.
BEV. *(She pours herself more wine.)* You want to, um, satisfy whatever you see. In his eyes, whatever that is. Where's Daddy is too complicated to get into. Who ever knows really? But men — that's an easier question to answer. They're everywhere! We just need one to come over the house every now and then.
REED. And what am I doing?
BEV. During daylight hours.
REED. I come over in the day! And the rest — the official — the title or formal title — there's no room for that. *(Beat.)* I don't know how to say this without —
BEV. Say it.
REED. — sounding meager —
BEV. No —
REED. — mean or —
BEV. *(Simultaneous with Reed's next line.)* — no — no — no — no — no — say it.
REED. — and I know we're supposed to be creating — I know all that, what you're trying to do here, everything you're building, and you two are great and totally sufficient I'm sure —
BEV. Say it!
REED. I am! I'm saying the whole thing sounds like a minefield.
BEV. Break it down.
REED. It's a minefield!
BEV. We need sturdiness, that's all I'm saying. And you're single now after Jason and we have these empty rooms — rent free by-the-by — and he's asking me where the men are. Rent-free and "Where are the men, Mommy?" and *rent-free.*
REED. Everything doesn't have to be a list.
BEV. It's not a list.
REED. Checking off things —
BEV. It's not a fucking list —
REED. — sconce, faucet, daddy! *(Beat.)* No, but I'm sorry.
BEV. I got it.
REED. No, I am, I'm sorry — some people don't get everything.
BEV. Okay, drop it.
REED. *(Beat.)* I just don't want it to come up again. Like I'm some-

how lacking. Like I'm some freak because I don't want children.
BEV. I thought you did — ?
REED. People who want children are the only people who should have them.
BEV. But you always said — ?
REED. I hated it, being young. I hated it. So what am I supposed to convey to a kid? And what about when do I get to be carefree? My mother — being the oldest, all that — when am I allowed to be — have my carefree time? I'm not gonna turn around just when I have some semblance of —
BEV. Fine.
REED. — freedom —
BEV. Fine.
REED. I'm not, I'm sorry — I am. It would work out well. It would.
BEV. It would.
REED. I know. But I don't want it. He's lovely, he's great. I have a crush, with his pictures, and I quote all his little things to people, his little things he says about poop and monsters, go around like some suburban mom saying Georgie said blah blah —
BEV. He's verbal.
REED. He's very verbal.
BEV. He is.
REED. I know, he talks. I'm saying he is. And I like that in a kid. I know what he's thinking. The ones who don't talk, they spook the fuck out of me! Staring there with their eyes, judging me or something, feeling superior, knowing I don't know shit, little devil children. Fuck them, they give me shivers. Hester Prynne's kid. The power they have. The power they have over you. *(Beat.)* Which can be ... fun. Sometimes. A kid can be a lot of ... It's just I — I wanted one with Jason.
BEV. Okay. *(Shelly comes in carrying a coffee-table book.)*
REED. *(To Shelly.)* I'm sorry.
SHELLY. Just think about it. We don't need a yes today. We're celebrating today. All we need to focus on is all the good that's happened. Everything in our lives. Going up. Getting what we've ever wanted. You are our best male friend. Here's the book. *(She hands it to Reed.)* It's about the Nubians. *(Referring to the wine bottle near*

22

Bev.) Did you open a bottle?
BEV. It's from the holidays. It was already.
SHELLY. That's old stuff. Let's open a new one. We have split somewhere. Veuve — *(She looks for it.)* — somewhere — Clicquot —
BEV. It was half-full still —
SHELLY. No, fine, we're celebrating, why not? *(To Reed.)* Take some time with it, tonight's a party.
REED. *(Beat.)* Do you mind if we have dinner another night? *(They don't. Reed smiles and goes. He returns home and lies down on his bed. His eyes are shut only a moment when Jason enters the room. Reed sits up, not knowing what to say. Jason paces before beginning.)*
JASON. You can't do that. You can't anymore. Calling me. And some set place. Some agreement we come to and showing up at a certain time only to — to — you can't. That's it. I don't want the keys anymore. *(He throws a set of keys on the floor.)* It's too easy. It's this thing that we should be sure we're thinking. I don't want to be in intimate situations and not have thought behind them. Not be conscious, not consciously know what we're doing. And fuck you! Fuck me? Fuck you! I am fine. I'm fine. I'm sitting there fine at my desk and you call and make plans?! Fuck you. Like nothing's happened. Six months now! Something's happened and fuck you. Everyone knows. My friends say this is nothing. No reason at all. You overreacted and then, what, I have to come meet you in some place you've found in what, Zagat's? And sit there and eat hummus? I don't like hummus, it dries me out! And I'm meeting you places like we're still together when we are not. And getting into this whole thing that you start — and I'm just getting clear in my head — you know — and every time I start to get clear you call me up. And I don't call you — you call me. I'm sitting there fine, at my desk doing well. Everyone there says my work is excellent. That's what they say and you call me. You call me …
REED. *(Beat.)* I didn't mean to. *(Beat.)* I just wanted to see you.
JASON. You shit. What about me? Those shirts, that closet full of shirts for who? No one else likes them. You're the only one who likes me in blues and purples!
REED. I'm sorry.
JASON. Shut up.
REED. You can say that.

JASON. Shut up, shut up. *(Jason reaches for Reed's hand. He then sits next to Reed on the bed.)* I don't want any of those pictures. Don't make copies for me. Vieques — I picked out the ones I like. That time in Atlanta, or upstate. Anything. Any of that. You know I don't collect things. I've left boxes everywhere and I forget what's in them and I never need them again. So don't track me down with souvenirs. Sentimental little kitschy little maudlin little things. That stuffed thing with the key chain, I don't need that. I've taken everything I need to take. If you, in the next months, a book, something turns up — I don't care. Salvation Army. Poor people can have those things. Give anything you find that's mine to someone who wants it. I don't. Things don't matter to me. *(He stands.)* Monday I'm going to Litchfield. One of our clients. This campaign we're presenting.
REED. Okay.
JASON. *(Beat.)* You don't know what you've done. Do you?
REED. No. Yes, I do. No.
JASON. *(Beat.)* I'm sorry. You have the keys back. I'm sorry. I miss — everything.
REED. So do I. I'm sorry.
JASON. Yeah. Yeah. *(Beat.)* If I — if I — if I do come back — *(Beat.)* If I come back. If I come back and we — are — here — I'm here — back here — there are, um —
REED. Okay.
JASON. Things.
REED. Okay.
JASON. That.
REED. Some — some — I know.
JASON. Things. Not — not — not —
REED. No.
JASON. Not just like on a, you know, the ways and means —
REED. No, yes, absolutely. No.
JASON. If I get my act together, see someone — therapy — whatever —
REED. Of course.
JASON. — and you — you — you have to do things! It's not just me. You think it's easy for me with you, all over creation? Sometimes for days —

REED. I know —
JASON. How flirty you are!
REED. *(Beat.)* What?
JASON. You know.
REED. You're flirty too!
JASON. You mean it, though, you mean it! Those assistants, those notes. "Thank you for this opportunity, I want to someday be who you are. I emptied the trash, too, even though you didn't ask me to — think more of me!" That little sprite from Chicago, are you serious?
REED. I —
JASON. Little post-its with stylized writing, calligraphy — that is inappropriate. It's unnecessary. Assistants should assist and get out. Help and get out. Don't help and flirt and leave little notes — you're twice his age.
REED. Oh, for God's sake —
JASON. No, no, you listen.
REED. I encouraged none of that.
JASON. No, no.
REED. He's ten years younger!
JASON. Oh, he's ten years —
REED. He's not *two times* —
JASON. That's an improvement.
REED. — you know, one-half my age for God's sake —
JASON. He's younger.
REED. They're all younger! They're assistants — that's why they're younger. And they'll always be younger because people keep making more of them. They'll never be older — only we will be!
JASON. That's just it —
REED. Because they're making less of us!
JASON. That's just it!
REED. *(Beat.)* You are the most beautiful — the most beautiful. Those notes — ? Some kid — ? You. Do you know who you are? Do you know when I think of you? What I think? You can't possibly think as much as me. *(Jason puts his head in Reed's lap.)* What about this new guy? This adult relationship you've been having. The one where you're all adult-ish.
JASON. Come on.

25

JASON. Okay.
JASON. What if we did have a child?
REED. What?
JASON. I want to have to be responsible. I'm ready.
REED. You do?
JASON. Everything we always talked about. I don't want to leave. Can we — can we talk and — and think — and try? A kid, Reed? Someone to raise. Better than we were. For our extra love? *(Beat.)* What? What is it?
REED. Yes.
JASON. Yes what? *(Reed looks toward Bev and Shelly's apartment. There Shelly finds Bev finishing a phone call.)*
SHELLY. Okay, let's not get excited.
BEV. I'm fine.
SHELLY. Don't get all excited.
BEV. You're the one who's up.
SHELLY. What did he say?
BEV. He said —
SHELLY. No, verbatim, the words.
BEV. Yes.
SHELLY. What exactly did he say? You were on the phone. Where was he?
BEV. On the phone.
SHELLY. No, calling from.
BEV. I don't know.
SHELLY. You don't know where he was calling from?
BEV. He was —
SHELLY. Come on.
BEV. He was calling from the other end of the line!
SHELLY. Okay, he was home probably and he said what?
BEV. He said yes.
SHELLY. Verbatim — yes, a firm yes?
BEV. A yes to —
SHELLY. And this was what time?
BEV. — to proceeding. He had questions. This was just before you came in.
SHELLY. And that's when? That's when?
BEV. You came in right in the middle. What — ?

SHELLY. When was that?
BEV. You came in! It was ten minutes ago.
SHELLY. Bev! Exactly?
BEV. I guess!
SHELLY. Good, so he must've been home. Good.
BEV. Yes.
SHELLY. He was in a place where decisions — surrounded by things, books, his things that remind him — pictures, family photos — of his life. Friends, vacations, in a good place, so this doesn't sound —
BEV. He was fine.
SHELLY. — capricious —
BEV. He was having a drink.
SHELLY. — or jumped-to. A drink of what?
BEV. Lemonade.
SHELLY. He said that?
BEV. Strychnine, I don't know. He said he'd taken the phone to the roof and it was hot —
SHELLY. On the roof?
BEV. — so he'd brought up something —
SHELLY. On the roof?
BEV. He's got that little deck thing.
SHELLY. I've never been there.
BEV. I could hear ice — and he said it was hot there.
SHELLY. What, a cocktail?
BEV. Oh, for Christ —
SHELLY. On the fucking roof?
BEV. I'm not going to have this conversation.
SHELLY. You heard ice in a glass on the roof?
BEV. Please, it was lemonade! It wasn't a "drink."
SHELLY. People put booze in lemonade.
BEV. He'd squeezed some —
SHELLY. They put vodka in, it's allowed!
BEV. It was a fucking power drink or something! He's working out — some fruit drink! There wasn't booze in it! It's nine A.M. for Chrissake!
SHELLY. That hasn't stopped him in the past!
BEV. Please.

SHELLY. Or you.
BEV. Here we go.
SHELLY. Him or you. In the past. If it was the morning — why not? The sun never stopped either of you! The sun in the morning never got in the way of anyone's cocktails in that group!
BEV. I'm not going to proceed if you're going to be all cunty. Do me the courtesy, please, of not being totally cunty. Please. You just turn into this raving, paranoid, twelve-foot cunt.
SHELLY. Forget the whole thing.
BEV. And two isn't a group.
SHELLY. What, please?
BEV. You called us a group.
SHELLY. Whatever.
BEV. Two isn't a group.
SHELLY. Well, it's something.
BEV. It certainly is.
SHELLY. Forget the whole thing.
BEV. He's coming over.
SHELLY. When? To talk to me?
BEV. You're half the battle.
SHELLY. That's good.
BEV. Tonight.
SHELLY. That's good.
BEV. Okay.
SHELLY. I'll smell his breath, for one. *(Beat.)* But good. Shows he's serious.
BEV. You're not going to smell his breath.
SHELLY. Shows he understands the seriousness. He wouldn't dare come over drunk. *(Beat.)* I know it was the past and I'm sorry.
BEV. He's changed for fuck's sake.
SHELLY. I know.
BEV. I've changed. I had to. And I did. Less — less — less — you know — more — more adult. I had to! I would have sooner or later. But I was impelled. Our relationship. What was being offered —
SHELLY. You know I'm grateful.
BEV. — what could be exponentially —
SHELLY. I am —

BEV. — more.
SHELLY. — and you don't know.
BEV. More all around.
SHELLY. You don't know. How grateful. I get up every morning and look at you asleep and think — ! You don't know I know. The faith you've had.
BEV. Thank you.
SHELLY. And I know.
BEV. *(Beat.)* He was good to me. Before you. Before you there was someone who was good to me, in his way. That should — and we shouldn't be threatened by those who loved our lovers before us. We should be — please — grateful.
SHELLY. When did you say he was coming?
BEV. He just said tonight.
SHELLY. Do we have anything in the fridge?
BEV. I said we'd go out for dinner.
SHELLY. Did we finish the pears?
BEV. No, we bought too many.
SHELLY. They're just going to rot if we don't eat them.
BEV. Let 'em rot!
SHELLY. *(Beat.)* And he said dinner?
BEV. I said we would pick a place and call so he could dress appropriately.
SHELLY. And where's Georgie?
BEV. On his play date.
SHELLY. Good. And when does the play date end?
BEV. It's open-ended until they get cranky. *(They hold hands.)*
SHELLY. Good.
BEV. Thank you.
SHELLY. Can we make love? It's been weeks.
BEV. Shell, everything we're doing —
SHELLY. I miss you.
BEV. I'm right here. I'm tired.
SHELLY. You sure? *(Beat.)* Okay.
BEV. We will.
SHELLY. Call him and tell him eight.
BEV. Can I call him in a bit? I need to take a walk. *(Bev goes out and Shelly follows. Across town, Jason comes into Reed's apartment,*

carrying a box.)
JASON. That's the last of it. For now.
REED. We can put them somewhere.
JASON. It's just clothes and necessary things.
REED. Right.
JASON. I mean, we can put them somewhere and hang a few things out of the way and —
REED. Great.
JASON. — and so then most of the stuff is still at my apartment — which is important.
REED. Yes!
JASON. I think it's important I keep it, right?
REED. Yes, absolutely!
JASON. I mean, I think that was part of the problem, that I didn't have anywhere to go — that was mine! I didn't have a place.
REED. No, I absolutely think so too! And that will be good for me.
JASON. Good.
REED. If I'm doing work at home and I'm spread out we won't be underfoot like we were — you're right.
JASON. Good.
REED. And I think that caused things to —
JASON. It wasn't good!
REED. Tensions.
JASON. I needed my own place. To have it, for once. And I like it. I've never had that. I'll probably never sleep there again but — *(They laugh.)* But it's there.
REED. I'm glad. I'm so — glad. *(Reed smooths Jason's hair.)*
JASON. Let's do something tonight.
REED. I've got the girls tonight.
JASON. Oh.
REED. Not all night.
JASON. Can I come?
REED. Uh —
JASON. Can you cancel?
REED. Not all night, there's just this thing we're working on they want to discuss and I said I would and that should be early. And then I'll come back and we'll go somewhere. Try that new place. Oxtail ceviche! Is this weird?

JASON. A little.
REED. I'm glad though.
JASON. *(Suddenly hugging Reed.)* Don't do that again. Please don't do that. Don't throw me out. You can't.
REED. Sweetie, I didn't —
JASON. No, I know, shhhh.
REED. Okay.
JASON. Shhh. Say you won't, even though that's what you didn't do.
REED. I won't.
JASON. Okay. *(Beat.)* And I'll put my stuff away, out of the way! I'll hang what I need to hang, and I'll only take a couple drawers.
REED. We should maybe get another dresser.
JASON. Really?
REED. I think, yeah!
JASON. Great, 'cause there was never enough room! And I won't put my papers everywhere, or anything on the floor — which I know you hate.
REED. It's just things on the floor gather dust bunnies.
JASON. I know!
REED. This ancient place!
JASON. I know and I'll put everything up. Up high. On surfaces! No books or papers on the floor. And I'll return my library books, I swear, on time so they're not everywhere.
REED. It's just such a small —
JASON. You're right.
REED. — space.
JASON. And if something needs to go, it goes. And if something needs to stay it does — or hang or something, then it will! And I want to meet your friends up at the house. Maybe not all at once, but — and I called that woman. That referral I got. She's a lot, she's not cheap, but my insurance covers twenty sessions at eighty percent, so I should be sane by then. *(They laugh.)*
REED. I could go with you. We could go together. To that one — or another one if you decide.
JASON. Um.
REED. If you decide you don't like her, you might not click right away, not everyone does.

JASON. I think —
REED. The last one — you were always distracted during the sessions by her white stockings — that's real. That happened. There's something that bugs you and the whole therapy is for nothing.
JASON. I think I'd like to try her alone.
REED. Okay.
JASON. For me. So I can tell her things.
REED. Sure.
JASON. If I need to. Things I might not feel —
REED. No, gotcha.
JASON. Okay?
REED. Absolutely.
JASON. Great.
REED. But what "things"?
JASON. Um.
REED. No, just please tell me, it's okay, of course, but for instance do you mean is everything new? Do we have to negotiate everything again or are we okay?
JASON. I don't —
REED. Or maybe should we maybe should see someone who could see the both of us? You with yours, your own, by yourself, and the both of us with someone else entirely. Because if this is suddenly a whole new deal maybe we need to clean slate and start right.
JASON. No —
REED. Some guidance —
JASON. Wait can we just go slow! Slower? I need to wait — and go slow. *(Beat.)* Can we take a nap? Do you have time to take a nap? I can unpack when you're gone?
REED. Really? *(They lie down together.)*
JASON. When we have a kid we won't be able to do this.
REED. And you're sure you want that?
JASON. Think of all the children who need fathers. Good ones. Wouldn't we be good ones? Yes.
REED. And what about William?
JASON. Shhhh … *(Jason falls asleep and Reed heads across town to Bev and Shelly's. As he enters their duplex, they greet him with big smiles.)*
SHELLY. Well. Hello.
REED. Hi.

BEV. *(Beat.)* I told her what you said. The gist.
REED. Hi.
SHELLY. Hello.
BEV. Can I get anything?
REED. No, no.
BEV. A pear?
SHELLY. We have cider. We bought too much when we had everyone over once the floors were done.
REED. They look great.
BEV. They were a bitch. So we had people over to dance on them.
SHELLY. You were out of town — which won't be a problem —
REED. Where was I?
SHELLY. We know that's part of your life. We travel too, so we know.
BEV. *(To Reed.)* Boston.
SHELLY. We only travel for vacation. Sometimes business. Rarely, but it happens. Mostly to get away and see things. Galapagos, the turtles. And Georgie loves it. Someday we'd like to do that with all of us.
REED. *(Correcting.)* Cambridge.
BEV. Cambridge, Boston, who cares, it's all just clean. *(They laugh.)*
REED. I had some questions.
SHELLY. Sure.
BEV. Before he says yes through and through.
SHELLY. We can say — right off the bat — okay — ?
REED. Uh — no, sure.
SHELLY. Right off the bat we know —
BEV. Maybe let him ask his first —
REED. No, no.
BEV. — and then you can respond.
SHELLY. Sure.
REED. It's okay if you know things off the bat, say it.
BEV. Can I say something?
SHELLY. Yes.
BEV. *(To Reed.)* Just because you know so much of this has been mulled over extensively. His life. In the future. What it should be, blah, blah, our hopes, blah, blah, plans for all of us — savings, schooling, the money in trust, blah blah — and so there are some

things we feel strongly about. And if there's —
SHELLY. Good.
BEV. Will you let me finish, please? And if there's to be any parent, guardian, big brother — whatever-we-call-it situation here, the rights — your rights — will have to be very carefully —
SHELLY. Exactly.
BEV. — thought out.
SHELLY. Good. Right. *(Off Bev.)* I thought you were finished.
BEV. I am, but how did you know that?
REED. Look.
SHELLY. You want anything?
REED. Cider would be great. *(Bev goes for it.)* Should I keep talking?
SHELLY. Sure.
REED. She's out of the room.
SHELLY. She catches up.
REED. I know there's a whole setup here, in place, and I don't want to disturb that. Of course I don't. *(Bev comes back with a glass of cider, which she hands to Reed.)* I was saying I don't want to disturb, or I wouldn't, anything that's already in place.
SHELLY. But you couldn't. You couldn't.
REED. What I mean —
SHELLY. You wouldn't be able to.
BEV. Okay. Please.
REED. I mean, I respect what's in place.
BEV. We know.
REED. But I am another person, added to the mix. And my life could change too.
SHELLY. *(Beat.)* Something's changed.
BEV. Will you let him —
SHELLY. You've gone back to Jason. *(Reed does not respond for a moment.)*
BEV. Reed?
REED. He's changed.
SHELLY. Oh, Christ.
BEV. Are you serious?
REED. He's been quite thoughtful and we've been having dinners. *(The women look at each other a moment.)* And he's seen, I

think, the error — not just of his, not just his — our ways. I've seen too. It's a two-way street —
BEV. Yeah, but —
REED. Although he caused most of it.
SHELLY. Are you kidding?
BEV. Reed —
REED. I allowed for it to happen — no, no — and you took my side because we're friends. That's why he's the baddy. He's not a real baddy! I allowed and created situations repeatedly. Not being diligent, last year, all that — I wasn't watchful! My father, the money, the work back to back. I melted. I just fucking melted.
SHELLY. He destroyed your life.
REED. And I let something go when I didn't know I was!
SHELLY. He's totally unreliable.
REED. I wasn't cognizant.
SHELLY. Worse!
REED. And I lost something. Something I've wanted back.
SHELLY. This changes things.
BEV. Wait.
SHELLY. Those nights —
BEV. Wait.
SHELLY. No, everything.
BEV. Okay.
SHELLY. Bev?
BEV. Okay, peace, everybody, one second. Let's not let our —
REED. He's changed.
BEV. — or run with —
SHELLY. It changes everything.
REED. That's why I wanted to come over.
BEV. *(After a beat, to Reed.)* Really? Are you really?
REED. He wants a child. To be responsible. To be less selfish.
SHELLY. Oh, shit.
REED. You've seen him with kids —
SHELLY. I knew this didn't make sense.
REED. — they love him. They fall asleep, like he's an angel. Georgie, that time, his first New Year's? Uptown after that day — his little head, Jason's shoulder. So soundly. He'd be a better father than I'd ever be. Two for one. This is a two-for-one sale.

SHELLY. No, it's not.
BEV. Reed.
SHELLY. I'm sorry. I'm sorry.
REED. *(Beat.)* Okay. *(Beat.)* No, okay, I figured.
SHELLY. We're sorry.
REED. I know.
SHELLY. But it still stands. Our offer.
REED. How? How can it?
BEV. Shell —
SHELLY. He's asking. *(To Reed.)* If — if things don't work out with Jason. Our offer stands.
REED. I love him.
SHELLY. It's about Georgie.
REED. I do. *(He starts to go. He stops before he's out.)* He makes me happy.
BEV. I know.
SHELLY. We know.
REED. I know he's — he makes me — I know but — happier than anyone.
SHELLY. He struggles, Reed.
BEV. Okay —
SHELLY. Right?
BEV. Okay!
SHELLY. No, there's a reason — !
REED. I know.
SHELLY. — his drinking, his depressions —
BEV. Okay, Shell —
SHELLY. — no, there's a reason —
REED. I know.
SHELLY. — no —
BEV. — okay, Shell —
SHELLY. — no, this revisionist —
REED. Okay.
SHELLY. — this idea that —
REED. No, no, no —
BEV. SHELL!
REED. No, she's RIGHT!
SHELLY. — that things — thank you — can change! Sometimes

they cannot. They can't. Sometimes they are bad and they stay that way. And then you cut your losses. You cut them. He's been proven time and time again. To be unreliable. To someone we love. And so he should be involved in raising a child?
BEV. *(To Shelly.)* But maybe things can. *(To Reed.)* Maybe he has. Shell? What if he has? And then all of us — there was a time when all of us —
SHELLY. I know.
BEV. — a brief time —
SHELLY. I know.
BEV. — we were happy. We were good.
SHELLY. That was then. And now there's — *(She points to Georgie's room.)* We have to think of him. He's who we're thinking of. All of us. No chances. A child. Us. Strength. Which will make everything clear. Wait. *(She listens.)* Shh, he's up.
BEV. *(Listens.)* He's up all right.
SHELLY. *(To Reed.)* Go into him.
BEV. *(Beat.)* Yeah, go in. *(Reed stands. He doesn't know what to do.)*
REED. We were happy.
SHELLY. You'll find someone.
BEV. *(Beat.)* You will, Reed.
SHELLY. Someone who is your equal. Who can give you a home.
BEV. He couldn't. Really. Which I want for you. And could he now? I don't know … But if you want to — to hold out — to hold out hope — we wouldn't — *(She looks to Georgie's room.)*
REED. You want me to go in?
SHELLY. Yes.
BEV. *(Beat.)* Go in and tell him polka dot isn't a color. *(Off Shelly.)* What? It's not. He should know. Polka dot is … two colors at the very least.
SHELLY. We think so much of you.
BEV. I always wanted to take you with me.
REED. Thank you.
SHELLY. You look like your father, when I met him.
REED. Thank you.
SHELLY. You had a good father. Everyone deserves that. *(Reed looks to his apartment. He can see Jason there. He goes to him, leaving the women without an answer.)*

JASON. You're early. I thought — are we having dinner? *(Reed realizes Jason is drunk.)* I had a little, but I'm okay. William called. *(Beat.)* I gave him this number. Is that okay? He's been good to me and I had to explain. But didn't know how. How do we explain all this back and forth? *(Beat.)* When do we land? Where we're safe? When are we where we never have to move from again?
REED. *(Beat.)* What?
JASON. *(Beat.)* Yeah.
REED. I can't do this again.
JASON. Sure. Sure. The minute things get tough. *(Reed starts to leave.)*
REED. I have to —
JASON. Fine, the minute things get tough. You want me to change but this is it! This is who I am and you love me! I am a drunk and that's who you love. You love a drunk. *(Reed goes.)* Everything's unpacked! And I am not a child! I AM NOT! *(Beat.)* Reed…? AND YOU SAID YOU WOULDN'T! YOU SAID YOU WOULDN'T DO EXACTLY WHAT YOU'RE DOING NOW! *(Beat.)* You said! *(Beat.)* I'm sorry. I'm so sorry. *(Reed returns to Shelly and Bev's apartment, where they have been waiting. When they see him they realize what's happened.)*
BEV. I'm sorry.
SHELLY. *(Beat.)* Do you want anything? *(Reed looks down the hall to Georgie's room.)* Go into him. He's still awake. Make sure his light is on. It's just as you go in. His doll is on the table. It's Curious George.
BEV. His favorite.
SHELLY. You'll need to know these things. *(After a moment Reed moves towards the child's room.)*

End of Act One

ACT TWO

June, the following summer. A beach. Bev and Reed, in bathing suits, occupy beach chairs. Bev is half-reading a book.

BEV. And then we'll get saltwater taffies.
REED. Excellent.
BEV. *(Beat.)* What's up your ass?
REED. Nothing.
BEV. It's just you're not so much fun.
REED. *(Beat.)* Nothing. *(Beat.)* I don't like the beach anymore. *(Beat.)* I've got jelly on my hands from Georgie's sandwich and its caked in my nails and includes salt now from the water. And I scratched myself somewhere that shall go unmentioned, and in the scratch now is salt with sugar from the jelly caked over where I itched forming a kind of irritating poultice.
BEV. *(Beat.)* Fine.
REED. A little inadvertent, some kind of Band-aid made from only irritating things.
BEV. Go back to the place.
REED. No.
BEV. Take a shower, have the place to yourself.
REED. No, then I will get a big lecture from Shelly and I'm not in the mood.
BEV. What lecture?
REED. Some diatribe about, you know, the need to be together at the beach.
BEV. Do you want to take a walk?
REED. My shoulders are burnt.
BEV. Keep your T-shirt on.
REED. The sun still comes through! I'm wearing forty-five and a reflective white T-shirt which should bounce the sun away in big

beams but it doesn't. And that's because of that totally inefficient car you bought. *(Beat.)* Yes. *(Beat.)* Yes, destroying the environment, yes. *(Beat.)* There's a reason the polar caps are melting and it's your fucking car! *(Beat.)* And every time we go for a walk we run into somebody. The last thing I want to do is run into somebody. "Hi!" And I always forget everyone's name. *(Beat.)* Maybe I'll make another sand castle.
BEV. *(Pointing to a sand castle out of view.)* This one is pretty good.
REED. It sucks. I didn't have enough water.
BEV. I'm gonna read my book. *(She does.)*
REED. *(Beat.)* Should we move the blanket because of the surf?
BEV. *(She looks at the surf.)* We've got another hour before we need to. *(She looks down the beach.)* Do you think he's okay down there?
REED. He's made some friends.
BEV. What kind of friends? Big friends?
REED. They look about average.
BEV. I mean are there bigger kids?
REED. Juergen is with him.
BEV. Good. I didn't see Juergen.
REED. He's there — *(He points to Juergen.)*
BEV. I see him. Good. *(Beat.)* You two seem to be getting along. You and Juergen.
REED. We have to.
BEV. I mean getting along more so. I'm not trying to make you self-conscious. I've just got my eye peeled. And I notice things. You two like each other or something. Which is okay.
REED. He smells like birdseed.
BEV. What?
REED. I don't like him, he smells like birdseed. So don't get all excited that we hooked up. It was only twice, so — don't go sending —
BEV. I'm just —
REED. — engraving —
BEV. — you two seemed —
REED. — engraved things —
BEV. — a few laughs —
REED. — wedding announcements —
BEV. — and time together —
REED. No one wants a lover who smells like birdseed! *(Beat.)*

And he's all interested in my feet. And I know that's very chic or something, feet are in, but get the fuck off my feet and come up to my torso once in a while. God forbid I should get kissed every now and then. I mean what ever happened to tonguing? It's like I'm at this especially ardent podiatrist's.
BEV. No one's saying anything. If you like him, great. If you don't, fine.
REED. I have to like him.
BEV. No, you don't.
REED. He's across the hall, we're sharing the same bathroom! I have to. *(Beat.)* I don't know what you even need him for.
BEV. You've been travelling a lot.
REED. I don't know why you need him. I've always travelled and suddenly Georgie needs something — a what? A nanny or —
BEV. Not a nanny.
REED. — something, whatever this guy —
BEV. A live-in.
REED. — this helper. When who am I?
BEV. We know who you are. Georgie knows. You're the guy who's always in Boston.
REED. *(Beat.)* Cambridge, please. You just do that to bug me.
BEV. Go down and play with them.
REED. No, my scrape hurts me.
BEV. Wash it off with the water.
REED. I just said —
BEV. The water in the cooler, you fag, the spring water. Wash the damn scrape off and go down and get in the game if you're feeling so out of it —
REED. I don't want to be "in the game." I am just commenting on the unnecessary need for the nanny.
BEV. You spend two nights letting him suck your toes, you'd think you'd have a friendlier take on things.
REED. *(Beat.)* I hope he doesn't expect that will continue. Is he expecting some big relationship or something?
BEV. He's a nice guy.
REED. Did he say something to you?
BEV. No.
REED. What — he has a fucking crush on me or something?

BEV. Just shut up and rinse your scrape.
REED. Oh, man, that's it. This is too weird. *(Beat.)* I can't rinse my scrape until I get home.
BEV. I'm reading my book now.
REED. I need iodine. *(Beat.)* I'm hungry. *(Beat.)* Where's Shelly with the burgers? I'm hungry. *(Beat.)* I'm sorry.
BEV. Then shut up.
REED. I'm ... unhappy.
BEV. *(Beat.)* There was probably a long line for the burgers.
REED. I'm sorry.
BEV. You don't have to keep saying that. *(Beat.)* Do you want to read my book?
REED. *(Beat.)* Yes, please. *(As Bev is about to hand over her book, Shelly approaches with a cardboard box full of burgers, fries, drinks, etc. ...)*
SHELLY. The kids they hire for the registers are idiots. These inbred — these local townies on god-knows-what. They just have to ring up fast food, but no. They have to talk to their little friends, they have to be slow — *(Looks for Georgie.)* Where are they?
BEV. *(Pointing to Georgie and Juergen.)* There.
SHELLY. There they are. Who are those kids? Those other kids? Those boys?
BEV. They're —
REED. Big, threatening older boys.
SHELLY. Who?
REED. Full of burgeoning testosterone.
BEV. They're those kids from across the patio, I think. Juergen's been with him.
SHELLY. Oh, fine.
REED. That should make it okay.
BEV. *(About Reed.)* He's cranky cause he's hungry. *(Shelly passes out the food.)*
REED. And my scrape has salt and jelly in it.
SHELLY. Wash it off.
BEV. He wants iodine.
SHELLY. I think Juergen's got some iodine in his things. *(She finds iodine in Juergen's things.)* Look at all this, my God. There's three different kinds of band-aids in here, sunblock, lotion,

Skintastic. This guy is unbelievably prepared.
REED. He's a boy scout.
SHELLY. What?
REED. It's their motto. "Prepare for the worst."
SHELLY. Juergen was a boy scout?
BEV. No —
SHELLY. That's not their motto.
REED. It should be.
SHELLY. *(Beat.)* Are you in a mood, Reed?
BEV. Okay —
REED. You were gone for two hours getting burgers!
SHELLY. Yeah, well, 'cause if you're in a mood —
REED. I just don't want Juergen up in my face. If you want a nanny or a helper or a boy scout with a foot fetish because I had to go to Cambridge twice in as many months for something you know — both of you — was crucial business for that project that Shelly knows she encouraged, if you need to then, I guess, want to somehow perversely punish me for something you totally understand because who knows why by hiring this guy that, yes, granted, I fucked twice, but mainly because he was in the bathroom when I wanted some water at two A.M., then fine. I will not complain. It's your life it's your child it's your money it's your home I am just some fag in a room. *(After a beat, Shelly douses him with her soda.)*
SHELLY. Don't talk to me like that. *(A moment passes. Reed is speechless. To Bev.)* I'm sick of him.
BEV. Oh, fuck. *(Another moment passes.)*
REED. *(To Shelly.)* You twat. *(After a beat, Shelly is on top of Reed. They grapple in the sand as Bev looks on, too stunned to intervene. Finally, Bev steps in and pulls Shelly from Reed. At this point, Jason comes from further down the beach. Seeing him, Shelly runs off. After a moment, Bev follows. It is only then that Reed sees Jason.)*
JASON. What happened?
REED. I got sand on me. *(They laugh. Jason points to Georgie.)*
JASON. He got big.
REED. He's almost five.
JASON. He's gonna be a bruiser. You look good.
REED. Thanks.
JASON. I'm fat.

REED. No.
JASON. It's okay.
REED. I always liked when you had a belly.
JASON. Well. Fading beauty.
REED. No, you have the bones. You'll always be good-looking. Your coloring.
JASON. You're all covered in sand!
REED. I think my foundation is shifting. *(Beat.)* How are — is things? How's everything?
JASON. Good. Yeah. We're up there — *(He points up the beach.)* About a hundred yards.
REED. Did you see us or were you just walking?
JASON. Come on, the whole beach was like, "Who's that dyke beating up that fag?" *(They laugh.)*
REED. Are you with people?
JASON. Yeah. William and some friends. We have a house. We got this summer. William got. He's been getting a lot of work and we wanted a place to come. You?
REED. Nobody.
JASON. I mean a place. Where you're staying.
REED. Right. With the girls. They still have their place. And they bought the lot next to it. They put in a court and, so, I can do that, for exercise. Bat a ball around.
JASON. So you're beach now? No more country?
REED. There were a few problems.
JASON. I'm sorry.
REED. Yeah. We all started sleeping with each other. It was pretty bloody there, at the end. So many people were sneaking into so many bedrooms that people lost track and actual couples kept crawling into bed with each other by mistake. Doors slamming, the wrong underwear, incriminating notes — very French farce. We're letting a court decide how the property splits. It's a mess. We can laugh about it sometimes. I can't believe I haven't run into you.
JASON. What's it been?
REED. Nine months. *(Beat.)* Are you happy?
JASON. *(Beat.)* Yes. *(Beat.)* You?
REED. *(Beat.)* No!
JASON. There's no one?

REED. A male nanny who smells like birdseed.
JASON. I've been seeing your picture.
REED. Yeah, well.
JASON. In magazines. I cut it out when I see it.
REED. You do?
JASON. I cut it out.
REED. *(Beat.)* What do you do with it? When you cut it out?
JASON. I save it. In a book you gave me.
REED. Which one?
JASON. Just one of them.
REED. Does William know?
JASON. Yes, yeah, he respects the, uh — I've always set out parameters with him, and he's always been, um, very respectful. We've been able to have our own lives and not meld into each other. And it's all more or less even.
REED. I think about you a lot.
JASON. Yeah?
REED. Uh-huh.
JASON. Why?
REED. Because I do. Because I miss you. And because I'm always — startled by how life can be so — awful. That — things haven't — found a way to work this out. I'm always, I'm always — amazed when life becomes so — awful! And I feel like I've been somewhere, or in a dream this year — a hold — um — a dream or fog since — *(Shelly runs back on and stops when she sees the two men.)*
SHELLY. *(To Reed.)* It's over. I want you out. Go back to your crazy ex — no one wants you in our house — *(Bev runs on, in tears.)*
BEV. Don't listen to her!
SHELLY. No, listen to me! You listen to me. You are out as of now. *(Reed stands, stunned. After a moment, he gathers his things and goes off.)*
BEV. *(To Shelly.)* Don't do this.
SHELLY. *(To Jason.)* And you too. I'm sick of all of you. The only one who's worth anything is Juergen. *(Jason goes off after Reed. Shelly looks out at the water.)* Where is he? I can't see them.
BEV. *(Pointing.)* They're there.
SHELLY. Where is my son!
BEV. THERE!

SHELLY. GOOD! Good. *(Reed arrives at a motel room, followed by Jason. Reed hasn't yet showered and is still a mess from the beach. He puts his things down and sits on the bed. Jason stands in the doorway.)*
JASON. There's cable.
REED. Great.
JASON. *(Beat.)* There's probably a Bible. We could read Leviticus.
REED. You don't have to stay.
JASON. Just till you get settled.
REED. I don't think I should. I think I should think where I go.
JASON. Didn't you keep your apartment?
REED. They found out I'd been subletting it.
JASON. Oh, no, I loved that place.
REED. You did not. You were always on about —
JASON. What? I was —
REED. — the light, the lack thereof, the roaches.
JASON. We took care of that.
REED. I know. But we were only roach-free a month when we broke up. So you didn't get to appreciate the roach-free environment.
JASON. My loss.
REED. It is! *(They laugh. And Jason comes into the room a bit — but still does not close the door.)*
JASON. I liked the fireplace, and the ivy on the wall, that wall. And the rooftops, out the window you could see.
REED. Yeah, well it's gone.
JASON. Do you want a soda?
REED. Nah.
JASON. We passed a machine.
REED. No, thanks.
JASON. There must be somewhere.
REED. Someone has a room somewhere. But recently I've been alienating people. People can suddenly only take so much of me. I always thought I was charming. Now I'm difficult.
JASON. This'll blow over.
REED. It's never really worked out. Georgie stares at me and I don't know what to say and everyone pretends I'm some sorta male figure when, really, I'm just a kind of very interesting boarder. Won't William be worried?
JASON. I called when you were checking in.

REED. Good. Sit or something. *(Jason sits on the bed.)*
JASON. He's out with friends tonight. They're going to this show I don't want to go to. Stand-up comics, telling anecdotes. Sketch comedy or improvisation or something. And I just hate it when people have to be funny. Some kid, you know, someone who was told he was funny in high school, selling out his family on stage with cute little stories, or something, his bathroom habits — any of that humor I hate. Bathroom stuff, body stuff, anything that has to do with the body or scabs or leakage. Once I saw this comedian do a whole riff about earwax and I was like, that's it, forget it. Pay all that to be mushed in with a bunch of assholes yukking it up with a two-drink minimum for, basically, liquor-flavored water?
REED. You don't like comics.
JASON. I don't. I like TV though. *(They laugh.)* Do you want to turn it on?
REED. Now?
JASON. I like TV. We could watch something.
REED. *(Beat.)* Is this weird?
JASON. What is?
REED. This —
JASON. Oh.
REED. You here.
JASON. Yeah, no, I just —
REED. Me covered in sand and —
JASON. Just a little.
REED. — is it bad?
JASON. No.
REED. I don't think I want to watch TV though.
JASON. Do you mind if I sit here a bit? *(Reed shakes his head and Jason sits.)*
REED. *(Beat.)* Tell me — tell me about him. You can tell me now. About him, please. William. All about him. It's okay. I think — I want to imagine — I'd like to hear your days.
JASON. No.
REED. I would. *(Jason collects his thoughts before proceeding.)*
JASON. He's — he's — he likes his work. He's a consultant on parks. How they should be arranged. Where the fountains go.
REED. Oh.

47

JASON. How they look at night with the lights, the shrubs, are there enough benches. Or too many. What style. We have all these models at home, little benches like in a doll house. He carves them. I move them around when he's late and I'm mad. And, you know, I didn't know people like him existed — I guess I thought there were just parks! But there are consultants on them and it's very precise and everybody comes in and dickers over everything for months and months, sometimes years. A lot of times years. There's one just got finished he took me to the week we met. And we had a picnic. *(Beat.)* I shouldn't —
REED. No. Please.
JASON. *(Beat.)* He's um — he's um —. I need water. *(He goes into the bathroom and continues from there.)* He's close to his family. And they're okay, they're Southerners. So they eat and say "y'all." I mean they're not hicks. They're not with pick-up trucks on cement blocks in the yard or anything. They're respectful and treat me like, um, when we've gone down, like some kind of dignitary. *(He returns with a glass of water.)* Some exotic person from a faraway place, you know, that they've been told they should treat well. And they do. And they do.
REED. Good.
JASON. Which is where he gets it. I don't want to do this if you're going to be sad.
REED. Why not?
JASON. I don't want to make you sad.
REED. It's a favor I need. How is the — the — the — when — the lovemaking?
JASON. Uh, no.
REED. No, please.
JASON. Forget it.
REED. Jason. Is he better than I was?
JASON. This is not fair.
REED. Is that why? No, please. How is this successful? How has it gone on? Why do you live in a house with someone who loves you and I'm in a room with a kid who stares? No one believes I'm a "role model." I don't have an apartment. Where will I go? I'm in fights with everyone, business is complicated — I daydream. I'm too old to daydream. And I hate Cambridge, all that colonial crap!

I was the first one of everyone to want a home and someone and then everyone got that and now I'm the last. Like musical chairs. Is he beautiful to you in bed?
JASON. *(Beat.)* Yes.
REED. And wasn't I?
JASON. You were.
REED. Wh — wh — are you still in therapy?
JASON. No.
REED. Do you still drink too much?
JASON. I —
REED. Do me this favor!
JASON. Yeah, I do! I do. Every now and then it's a mess. Every few months there's a night when he has to pick me up from somewhere, some stranger's, some bar I found I wouldn't be caught dead in, but there I am, puke on my shoes — we don't talk about it. That's the deal. That's what's implicit.
REED. Was I wrong?
JASON. No. About what?
REED. To want more?
JASON. I couldn't — I couldn't bear — I couldn't — please — I always — no, you weren't. I was just used to myself by then. And you asked me to change. And there's been —
REED. I know —
JASON. — too much —
REED. Believe me.
JASON. — change! *(He tries not to cry.)* So I couldn't elect to have more. I've only been able to keep up with —
REED. I know.
JASON. — William doesn't make me change. He lets me be. He doesn't need much. He takes care of himself. And I take care of me. *(Beat.)* I should go and you should wash that sand off.
REED. I have a scratch. I think it's infected.
JASON. Where?
REED. In a not-so-great place. There's no name for where it is.
JASON. Let me see. *(After a moment, Reed opens the top of his bathing suit. He indicates where the scratch is. Jason looks at it.)* You have to clean it.
REED. It hurts. No, it really hurts. Maybe we should go to a hos-

pital. My eyes water every time I move the slightest bit.
JASON. I'll clean it. But you'll have to be still. I'll do it.
REED. *(Beat.)* You will?
JASON. Can you be still while I do that?
REED. I think so. *(Jason moves toward him.)* We can't have sex, I have an open wound. *(Jason continues to move toward Reed. Back in the city, morning begins and Shelly is found at her office, talking on the phone.)*
SHELLY. Hi, Mom, it's me. I wanted to go over the plans for your trip. I have the itinerary here. Because I paid for the tickets. I can send you a copy. It's just how they do it. It's just how it's done and there won't be confusion at the airport, no. I'll send you everything in advance. You'll have it on your person. So you're flying into Rome. No, it's just outside the city, it's — mmm — *(She looks.)* — it's called da Vinci, it's near the beach and then you — no, you're staying in the city in Trastevere. If Daddy wants to bring his bathing suit, fine, but Rome doesn't have a beach and the hotel doesn't have a pool. Should I be relaying all this to him, instead? Fine. You're welcome. You're welcome. You don't have to keep thanking me. Really, Mom, stop or we'll have to talk later. You sent me that jelly as a thank you and I don't have time for all this gratitude. And I think — you know what I think? Forget it. No — you know what I think? It's some fucked-up way of making me feel guilty somehow for being able to treat you and Dad so well. Just accept it and be grateful, tell your friends and don't keep feeling the need to express this forced gratitude. *(She listens.)* She's fine. He's fine, he has the sniffles. Well, it's his birthday soon and then you can come over. No, he's on a business trip in Vancouver. He's been overextended a bit lately and he's been gone a lot and — no. We've hired someone. A nice guy who has training. He's Swiss so he keeps everything running. I know you like Reed, everyone likes Reed, but we need this professional who's more consistent. That is what is important for a child. *(She listens.)* Good, so everything's working out and you fly into Rome and from there a bus to Umbria. Which is beautiful. It's where Bev and I — when we first met and we couldn't afford Tuscany. I was still working downtown and Bev was waitressing and we thought, okay, so not Tuscany, but someday! And then Umbria. So beautiful. How could Tuscany be better? And

we thought maybe we found a, uh, new place. A new way. To do things. Based on disappointment. Which sets you off to someplace … unimagined … and — and — and — she's left me, Mom. She took Georgie. We were at the beach. I don't know what I've done. I yelled at Reed but I don't — I don't think that's it. It's been — I don't know what to do — we haven't been sleeping together and — what do I do? Mom? Mommy? *(She listens.)* Uh-huh. Uh-huh. Uh-huh. Okay. No, okay. Okay, sure. Then — have a good trip. No, we don't need to talk before you go. I'll have Sonia send you all the info. She's my new assistant. She puts up with me, but I think it's 'cause I pay her. I just wanted everything you had with Daddy. That's all. Okay. Send him my love. And — and — to you too. *(She hangs up the phone, puts some papers in a leather satchel, and makes a call to the outer office.)* Sonia? I'll be taking work home. I'd just rather be there today. Thank you. And Sonia? I just want to say you've been working out very well. Thank you for that. *(She hangs up and goes home. She finds Bev there, packing things.)*
BEV. There were some things I needed.
SHELLY. Of course.
BEV. Why aren't you at work?
SHELLY. I couldn't concentrate. This new assistant is always hovering.
BEV. Georgie's been asking for you.
SHELLY. Tell him I was asking for him. Tell him, please, I said I love him.
BEV. I do.
SHELLY. Good. How are you?
BEV. I'm okay. I'll just be a few minutes.
SHELLY. No, of course.
BEV. And Reed will be coming up in a minute. He's parking the car. To help me with some things.
SHELLY. Who's got Georgie?
BEV. He's at my mother's. Probably on some sugar high. *(They smile.)*
SHELLY. She spoils him.
BEV. Everyone does. He's beautiful. He misses you.
SHELLY. I'm having my attorney arrange a temporary schedule, I didn't want you to be surprised by it — visiting — just so it's

down on paper.
BEV. Of course. Absolutely. I expected. And we need to be comfortable with things.
SHELLY. I might have to let Juergen go. I didn't know what to tell him — or how long this might be, or if ever — if it would be — ever resolved. He has a list of people who wanted him if he was ever free. Imagine — to be so in demand. I said I'd be happy to keep paying him, but that wasn't the point. He wants to be doing his job, not sitting around reading magazines. He's one of those people who loves his work, which is children. And that's nice. *(Reed comes in. He nods at Shelly when he sees her.)*
REED. The car's by the curb.
SHELLY. Hi.
REED. Hi. *(Jason enters. Shelly looks at Bev.)* I thought we could use some help lifting.
SHELLY. Are you taking the fridge?
REED. No —
BEV. No, boxes —
JASON. I'll wait on the —
BEV. No. Come in.
SHELLY. Please. *(Jason comes in. A moment passes when no one knows what to say.)* I'll be in the office. *(She goes to her office. Another moment passes in silence. Bev resumes packing, and then Shelly returns.)* I need to do some reading so if you could keep the noise to a minimum.
BEV. Sure — ?
SHELLY. And does anyone want anything?
REED. No —
BEV. No.
SHELLY. There's a fridge full of things that have gone uneaten. So you might as well pack up as much as you want.
BEV. I can buy groceries.
SHELLY. What?
BEV. *(Beat.)* It's just I don't need to take your groceries.
SHELLY. *(Beat.)* They were things we bought last week.
BEV. I know.
SHELLY. *(After a beat, about Jason.)* Why is he here?
BEV. Jason is putting us up.

SHELLY. Oh.
BEV. Which is sweet.
SHELLY. *(Beat.)* I'm just surprised.
BEV. Why?
REED. He lives in a big house. *(After a beat, Shelly returns to her office.)*
BEV. I just need to get some things. *(Bev puts down what she's doing and goes into Shelly's office.)*
SHELLY. *(Off.)* I can't believe —
BEV. *(Off.)* Is there somewhere you can go — ?
SHELLY. *(Off.)* — traipsing in —
BEV. *(Off.)* — until I'm done —
SHELLY. *(Off.)* — those two —
BEV. *(Off.)* — the deli —
SHELLY. *(Off.)* — who are they — ?
BEV. *(Off.)* — or a cafe or a deli — ?
SHELLY. *(Off.)* I want them out.
BEV. *(Off.)* Then call your attorney.
SHELLY. *(Off.)* Right, Jason has a big house!
BEV. *(Off.)* You heard me, call your fucking attorney. *(Bev returns to the room and immediately resumes packing; Shelly is on her heels.)*
SHELLY. Can the boys go so we can talk?
BEV. They're helping me.
SHELLY. I don't want us to yell. Please.
BEV. We can talk tonight on the phone if you want, after Georgie's off.
SHELLY. Okay. Okay. *(Turns to Jason.)* I'm sorry. *(Beat.)* Where do you live now, Jason? *(Jason looks to Bev to see if it's okay; Bev nods.)*
JASON. We have a house in town and one on the island.
SHELLY. Who's "we"?
JASON. William. He's —
REED. His boyfriend.
BEV. That's where we're staying, so we have to go all the way out there, so we have to get on the road before the rush.
SHELLY. And — you're all — staying there?
BEV. Yes.
SHELLY. Everyone and you and the new lover and the old one?
JASON. William is out of town.

SHELLY. What does Georgie make of all this?
REED. What?
SHELLY. This little group, this hodgepodge.
BEV. It's hardly —
SHELLY. This upheaval. It's just pretty unconventional. *(After a beat, to Reed.)* You, your ex, his present —
REED. He's not —
SHELLY. — no Juergen, no me — or what do you make of all this? Very convenient isn't it? Almost perfect, almost pre-me, when it was just the three of you on one big party, waking up at noon, figuring out who'd pick up the bill later — those were the days! Except — you can't go back.
BEV. That's it.
SHELLY. That's right, Reed. You can't go back.
REED. What — ?
BEV. Forget this.
SHELLY. Yeah!
BEV. Come on!
SHELLY. No, you can't because his "present" who — his whoever-his-name — who's probably footing the bill too, right?
JASON. He's generous.
SHELLY. Sure!
BEV. We're not —
SHELLY. No, you're not! Why should you? Health insurance? Fuck that! If you're dead in a ditch — who cares! Let someone else get the bills! Broken glass! Picking it out of your hands — out of your hands! As my friends watched! Mortified for me — a dinner honoring me and you have glass imbedded in your palm and these two completely helpless, drunk themselves, and everyone around me — everyone! — saying who is this investment, Shelly? Who is this child you are marrying? My defenses on your behalf! Defending this and I'm glad we're here and you're with the boys, which is where you wanted! And go be with them but I will take our son. He will not become like them, you will not make him that. Do you hear me? I will do everything in my power to keep him from that.
BEV. *(Beat.)* I gave birth to him.
SHELLY. *(Beat.)* Go, take your things which I paid for. Eat your own groceries, wake up on Tenth Avenue where I found you — all

of you. *(She leaves the apartment. A moment passes.)*
REED. We'll go to Jason's. We can stay there as long as we want. We'll light a fire. Georgie likes that. Lawyers will be later. She'll cool down. This is the worst for someone like her. And she's wrong. We've all changed. She's not fair to — the past? She's always been jealous —
BEV. I know.
REED. Okay? Get your things and we'll do here.
BEV. Okay. *(She goes into the bedroom.)*
REED. When does William get back?
JASON. Not for a bit.
REED. So it's just us.
JASON. Yeah, for a bit.
REED. And Georgie.
JASON. For a month about.
REED. A whole month! I thought we could go tubing. And there's a couple of house tours I thought you might know about. And some friends, too, out there I never get to see who always ask about you. Is it weird again?
JASON. Yes. Isn't it?
REED. But not bad.
JASON. No!
REED. Like a reprieve. Who gets that?
JASON. No one. But here's the thing.
REED. Uh-huh?
JASON. Which is something I've been meaning to bring up.
REED. We're sharing costs, she's wrong. We'll pool everything and no one will be out of pocket.
JASON. No, it's when the month's up William will be back from Europe a few days.
REED. We'll go someplace else then. We've got time to look, that's how this is helpful —
JASON. Yes, but then I go back with him. We're moving there. He's got a job near Bordeaux, there's a park that dates back centuries and it's very prestigious, a contest actually he's won, people competing from all over. It was such a remote chance he'd get as far as he got, but it was his model that put him over. They all looked at it and just said, "Wow." He'd done the whole thing himself, he was pulling

all-nighters molding this fountain — I had to keep bringing him tea. And a French garden is a real coup and something he has only a little of on his resume. It's a special, you need a special ability to respond to a paradigm that's so cultivated, so precise. And it really appeals to him. And he speaks French, I don't know if I mentioned.
REED. You brought him tea.
JASON. And it's always been a dream of mine, France. I've been reading up on everything about it now that I'm in this groove at work, so I have time. To read.
REED. I know that makes you happy.
JASON. It does. And there's a child that we'll be adopting. We didn't know and we'd been waiting and he — he's a boy — finally came through. He finally came through.
REED. My God.
JASON. I know.
REED. I've wanted that for you.
JASON. So this — this has been in the works for some time now.
REED. So we have a month.
JASON. Uh-huh.
REED. It'll be July then.
JASON. We have till July.
REED. I was looking forward to July.
JASON. You still can. Right? *(Beat.)* Are you back on biographies yet?
REED. No.
JASON. I'm reading one on de Gaulle. *(After a moment, Bev returns with some bags.)*
BEV. We should get going.
JASON. Yeah, if we wait another minute the drive will be terrible. *(Jason picks up a bag and goes. Reed picks up another bag and follows. Bev looks around a moment, then goes out and catches up with the boys. Jason exits off as Reed and Bev continue into a suite of rented rooms.)*
REED. That should be it.
BEV. Well.
REED. Yup. *(They look around.)*
BEV. This is a shithole.
REED. It's where businessmen stay. It rents by the week, so we can camp out till we find a place.

BEV. For businessmen and those who love them.
REED. All work and obviously no play.
BEV. Nope. It needs a woman's touch. So you should get busy —
REED. Then I should get busy. *(Beat.)* It's all I could find with a separate room.
BEV. No, we're fine. You think he's asleep?
REED. I checked him ten minutes ago. He felt a little warm, but I think it's from the day.
BEV. I'll check him.
REED. You might check him in a bit. And we need to get his cereal. He was all in a panic about Count Chocula. Or I can run to the market, but I've only got — *(He empties his pockets and produces some bills.)* Is this enough for Count Chocula?
BEV. Wait, I've got — *(She empties her pockets and they pool the money.)* That should do us.
REED. There's got to be an ATM somewhere.
BEV. And get some coffee for the morning.
REED. Good thinking.
BEV. We'll need it.
REED. And the paper.
BEV. Anything in the fridge? *(Reed goes off to see.)*
REED. *(Off.)* Half a bottle of blush.
BEV. Eww.
REED. *(Off.)* Want a glass?
BEV. Why not? *(Reed returns with the blush and two glasses. He pours a glass for Bev.)* Not that much. *(They sit and toast and drink.)*
REED. What is blush anyway?
BEV. White wine that feels ashamed. *(Beat.)* What are you thinking about?
REED. What are you thinking about?
BEV. Georgie. He seemed a little girly on the playground today. He wanted to play outfield but he kept running away from the ball.
REED. So he'll cut hair. *(Beat.)* Wait.
BEV. What?
REED. We're sleeping on the couch?
BEV. You said it pulls out.
REED. You aren't going to pee in your sleep?
BEV. On a half a glass of wine?

REED. Okay!
BEV. That happened once and you keep bringing it up like I'm ready for diapers!
REED. I like that it makes you cranky.
BEV. Well it does! *(Beat.)* I like it actually, too. I only peed that once though. And you've spun it into this decades-long loose bladder story. *(Beat.)* And I was sleeping when it happened. It's not like I elected to whiz on the furniture. It was not premeditated pee. And to this day everyone I know starts shaking when they pour me wine! I saw Marci pat the sofa once after I got up. It's not fair. I don't have a pee story for you. *(They laugh.)*
REED. Let's come up with one!
BEV. *(Beat.)* And it's not like I ever drank all that much.
REED. Please, you drank like it was your job. *(Beat.)* Whatever happened to her?
BEV. Who?
REED. That girl whose sofa you relieved yourself on?
BEV. It was a chaise, actually. See, always embellishing.
REED. She was funny. I liked her.
BEV. She's in the Northwest somewhere. Probably with plastic all over the upholstery. *(Beat.)* She left me when I met you.
REED. She was threatened. Were you threatened when I met Jason?
BEV. Sure. At first. Then I found Shelly. And then were you threatened?
REED. Still am.
BEV. Me too.
REED. *(Beat.)* No. I was glad. 'Cause things evened out. We went from a two-legged beast to a three-legged one, so we needed a fourth.
BEV. So we didn't really break up, I guess.
REED. Who?
BEV. Us.
REED. One night is hardly a relationship. I mean, that's how I do the math.
BEV. Yeah, but two times though. It wasn't a bad night.
REED. I was feeling sexual. In a way that, you know, that could've been directed at anything.
BEV. Thanks.

REED. Aim and fire.
BEV. Thanks a lot.
REED. You know I don't mean that.
BEV. *(Raising her glass.)* You weren't inept.
REED. *(Raising his.)* You weren't grossed out.
BEV. You kidding? I liked guys till I was twenty-four. Then I just got pussy crazy.
REED. I never got that. But it didn't seem — it seemed — we were comfortable, and it seemed like we were, um, doing each other a favor.
BEV. We were curious.
REED. The sweetest favor.
BEV. We were drunk.
REED. Curious like kids. We'd had a lot, it's true.
BEV. *(Looks off to Georgie's room.)* He'll be there someday. *(Yawns and looks at her glass.)* See? I can't do it anymore.
REED. I'm about ready myself — *(He looks at the sofa.)* I wonder how this thing pulls out. *(They both unfold the sofa bed.)*
BEV. There. *(They undress. They look at each other. They look at the bed.)*
REED. Should we check on him?
BEV. He's flushed from the sun is all.
REED. *(Beat.)* Should we go to bed?
BEV. Yes. You first.
REED. Okay.
BEV. Shouldn't you go to the market though?
REED. We can do that in the morning. We'll go together.
BEV. Thank you. *(He steps into the bed. She follows. He turns out the light. They lie face up in bed, silent for a long, long moment.)* What's gonna happen?
REED. When it comes to things like this … I'm not sure. *(They begin to move toward each other as the lights go out.)*

End of Play

PROPERTY LIST

Martini shaker and two martini glasses (REED)
Gift-wrapped book (JASON)
Watch (REED)
Glass of wine (BEV)
Papers (SHELLY)
Open bottle of wine (BEV)
Coffee-table book (SHELLY)
Keys (JASON)
Phone (BEV)
Box (JASON)
Glass of cider (BEV)
Book (BEV)
Blanket (REED)
Cardboard box with burgers, fries, drinks (SHELLY)
Iodine, bag (SHELLY)
Beach bag (REED)
Glass of water (JASON)
Office phone (SHELLY)
Leather satchel, papers (SHELLY)
Suitcase, clothes (BEV)
Duffel bags or suitcases (BEV)
Money (REED, BEV)
Open bottle of blush, two glasses (REED)

NEW PLAYS

★ **MONTHS ON END by Craig Pospisil.** In comic scenes, one for each month of the year, we follow the intertwined worlds of a circle of friends and family whose lives are poised between happiness and heartbreak. "...a triumph...these twelve vignettes all form crucial pieces in the eternal puzzle known as human relationships, an area in which the playwright displays an assured knowledge that spans deep sorrow to unbounded happiness." *–Ann Arbor News.* "...rings with emotional truth, humor...[an] endearing contemplation on love...entertaining and satisfying." *–Oakland Press.* [5M, 5W] ISBN: 0-8222-1892-5

★ **GOOD THING by Jessica Goldberg.** Brings us into the households of John and Nancy Roy, forty-something high-school guidance counselors whose marriage has been increasingly on the rocks and Dean and Mary, recent graduates struggling to make their way in life. "...a blend of gritty social drama, poetic humor and unsubtle existential contemplation..." *–Variety.* [3M, 3W] ISBN: 0-8222-1869-0

★ **THE DEAD EYE BOY by Angus MacLachlan.** Having fallen in love at their Narcotics Anonymous meeting, Billy and Shirley-Diane are striving to overcome the past together. But their relationship is complicated by the presence of Sorin, Shirley-Diane's fourteen-year-old son, a damaged reminder of her dark past. "...a grim, insightful portrait of an unmoored family..." *–NY Times.* "MacLachlan's play isn't for the squeamish, but then, tragic stories delivered at such an unrelenting fever pitch rarely are." *–Variety.* [1M, 1W, 1 boy] ISBN: 0-8222-1844-5

★ **[SIC] by Melissa James Gibson.** In adjacent apartments three young, ambitious neighbors come together to discuss, flirt, argue, share their dreams and plan their futures with unequal degrees of deep hopefulness and abject despair. "A work...concerned with the sound and power of language..." *–NY Times.* "...a wonderfully original take on urban friendship and the comedy of manners—a *Design for Living* for our times..." *–NY Observer.* [3M, 2W] ISBN: 0-8222-1872-0

★ **LOOKING FOR NORMAL by Jane Anderson.** Roy and Irma's twenty-five-year marriage is thrown into turmoil when Roy confesses that he is actually a woman trapped in a man's body, forcing the couple to wrestle with the meaning of their marriage and the delicate dynamics of family. "Jane Anderson's bittersweet transgender domestic comedy-drama ...is thoughtful and touching and full of wit and wisdom. A real audience pleaser." *–Hollywood Reporter.* [5M, 4W] ISBN: 0-8222-1857-7

★ **ENDPAPERS by Thomas McCormack.** The regal Joshua Maynard, the old and ailing head of a mid-sized, family-owned book-publishing house in New York City, must name a successor. One faction in the house backs a smart, "pragmatic" manager, the other faction a smart, "sensitive" editor and both factions fear what the other's man could do to this house— and to them. "If Kaufman and Hart had undertaken a comedy about the publishing business, they might have written *Endpapers*...a breathlessly fast, funny, and thoughtful comedy ...keeps you amused, guessing, and often surprised...profound in its empathy for the paradoxes of human nature." *–NY Magazine.* [7M, 4W] ISBN: 0-8222-1908-5

★ **THE PAVILION by Craig Wright.** By turns poetic and comic, romantic and philosophical, this play asks old lovers to face the consequences of difficult choices made long ago. "The script's greatest strength lies in the genuineness of its feeling." *–Houston Chronicle.* "Wright's perceptive, gently witty writing makes this familiar situation fresh and thoroughly involving." *–Philadelphia Inquirer.* [2M, 1W (flexible casting)] ISBN: 0-8222-1898-4

DRAMATISTS PLAY SERVICE, INC.
440 Park Avenue South, New York, NY 10016 212-683-8960 Fax 212-213-1539
postmaster@dramatists.com www.dramatists.com

NEW PLAYS

★ **BE AGGRESSIVE by Annie Weisman.** Vista Del Sol is paradise, sandy beaches, avocado-lined streets. But for seventeen-year-old cheerleader Laura, everything changes when her mother is killed in a car crash, and she embarks on a journey to the Spirit Institute of the South where she can learn "cheer" with Bible belt intensity. "...filled with lingual gymnastics...stylized rapid-fire dialogue..." –*Variety*. "...a new, exciting, and unique voice in the American theatre..." –*BackStage West*. [1M, 4W, extras] ISBN: 0-8222-1894-1

★ **FOUR by Christopher Shinn.** Four people struggle desperately to connect in this quiet, sophisticated, moving drama. "...smart, broken-hearted...Mr. Shinn has a precocious and forgiving sense of how power shifts in the game of sexual pursuit...He promises to be a playwright to reckon with..." –*NY Times*. "A voice emerges from an American place. It's got humor, sadness and a fresh and touching rhythm that tell of the loneliness and secrets of life...[a] poetic, haunting play." –*NY Post*. [3M, 1W] ISBN: 0-8222-1850-X

★ **WONDER OF THE WORLD by David Lindsay-Abaire.** A madcap picaresque involving Niagara Falls, a lonely tour-boat captain, a pair of bickering private detectives and a husband's dirty little secret. "Exceedingly whimsical and playfully wicked. Winning and genial. A top-drawer production." –*NY Times*. "Full frontal lunacy is on display. A most assuredly fresh and hilarious tragicomedy of marital discord run amok...absolutely hysterical..." –*Variety*. [3M, 4W (doubling)] ISBN: 0-8222-1863-1

★ **QED by Peter Parnell.** Nobel Prize-winning physicist and all-around genius Richard Feynman holds forth with captivating wit and wisdom in this fascinating biographical play that originally starred Alan Alda. "QED is a seductive mix of science, human affections, moral courage, and comic eccentricity. It reflects on, among other things, death, the absence of God, travel to an unexplored country, the pleasures of drumming, and the need to know and understand." –*NY Magazine*. "Its rhythms correspond to the way that people—even geniuses—approach and avoid highly emotional issues, and it portrays Feynman with affection and awe." –*The New Yorker*. [1M, 1W] ISBN: 0-8222-1924-7

★ **UNWRAP YOUR CANDY by Doug Wright.** Alternately chilling and hilarious, this deliciously macabre collection of four bedtime tales for adults is guaranteed to keep you awake for nights on end. "Engaging and intellectually satisfying...a treat to watch." –*NY Times*. "Fiendishly clever. Mordantly funny and chilling. Doug Wright teases, freezes and zaps us." –*Village Voice*. "Four bite-size plays that bite back." –*Variety*. [flexible casting] ISBN: 0-8222-1871-2

★ **FURTHER THAN THE FURTHEST THING by Zinnie Harris.** On a remote island in the middle of the Atlantic secrets are buried. When the outside world comes calling, the islanders find their world blown apart from the inside as well as beyond. "Harris winningly produces an intimate and poetic, as well as political, family saga." –*Independent (London)*. "Harris' enthralling adventure of a play marks a departure from stale, well-furrowed theatrical terrain." –*Evening Standard (London)*. [3M, 2W] ISBN: 0-8222-1874-7

★ **THE DESIGNATED MOURNER by Wallace Shawn.** The story of three people living in a country where what sort of books people like to read and how they choose to amuse themselves becomes both firmly personal and unexpectedly entangled with questions of survival. "This is a playwright who does not just tell you what it is like to be arrested at night by goons or to fall morally apart and become an aimless yet weirdly contented ghost yourself. He has the originality to make you feel it." –*Times (London)*. "A fascinating play with beautiful passages of writing..." –*Variety*. [2M, 1W] ISBN: 0-8222-1848-8

DRAMATISTS PLAY SERVICE, INC.
440 Park Avenue South, New York, NY 10016 212-683-8960 Fax 212-213-1539
postmaster@dramatists.com   www.dramatists.com